Caught in the Storm

F-Pentatonic Series Book 3

Jai Schelbach

Andrés González

Copyright © 2021 Jai Schelbach
Caught in the Storm: Self-published
jaischelbach@gmail.com
www.jaischelbach.com
All rights reserved.
No part of this publication may be reproduced, stored in a retrieval system, stored in a database and / or published in any form or by any means, electronic, mechanical, photocopying, recording or otherwise, without the prior written permission of the publisher.
ISBN: 978-0-6488904-7-8
Hardcover edition

Dedicated to:

My daughter, Evie. You light up my life and fill me with such happiness. Your smile, your big heart and your kindness are qualities that can calm any storm!

On the Jackson's Farm
down Wildflower Lane
lived a turtle called Tom,
whose life was mundane.
Till one sunny day,
a few months ago,
he learned to read music,
three notes on his own.
D on line 4,
C on space 3,
A on space 2,
he was starting to read.
Now some time had passed
when one strange day
a menacing storm
came drifting his way.

The clouds they bellowed
the lightening it flared,
the thunder cried out,
"Watch out, beware!"
As the rain pelted down,
the waterline rose
the creek started flooding
and swiftly it flowed.
Without hesitation
Tom took to the hills,
up the old track
past the broken-down mill.

As Tom fled to safety,
the weather closing in,
He heard a shout
in that racket and din.
It was then that he spied
through the blurry haze,
a lizard on a leaf
who was floating away.
Tom spun around
to the rescue he dashed
to save the poor lizard
who frantically splashed

Into the torrent
He swam strong and swift
yelling, "Jump on my shell
I can give you lift."
But as the lizard
climbed onto his back

a log floated by
hitting Tom with a WHACK!
His vision went blurry,
He started to sink,
when all of a sudden...

lights out with a CLINK!

(what do you think happened to Tom?)

Tom opened his eyes
slowly he blinked
face-to-face with a lizard
all speckled and pink
"Where am I? What's happened?
And who are you?"
Tom stammered as his world
slowly came into view.
"I'm Griffin the Gecko
and you just saved me
with courage you swam
through the flood and debris."

"As I was climbing
onto your back
a log came along
and gave you a WHACK!!!
We tossed and turned
our situation was dire,
we tumbled and turned
like clothes in a dryer.
Then right at that moment,
with one foot in the grave,
a small paper boat
came riding the waves.
I thrashed in the water
till I reached the boat's side,
I climbed in the vessel
just glad to be alive.
But you drifted past me
floating upside down
I grabbed onto your shell
so you wouldn't drown.

Pulling you in
we were safe at last
then I set course for shore
whilst rubble streamed past."
We dodged a branch,
And a half eaten plum,
Then docked on the shore
Near a old rusty drum.
Pulling you onto
the damp, soggy ground,
I waited and slowly
you came around."

Tom coughed a little,
before clearing his throat.
"Thank you" he said
"For keeping us afloat."
Then noticing the boat
washed up by the tide
he spotted a symbol
on the paper boats side.
Unfolding the paper
in the drizzling rain
they were full of excitement
to see what it contained.

"What does it say?"
said Griffin to Tom
"It says 'Ickle Ockle',
in fact it's a song."
Tom started to sing,
with a smile on his face,
but was stopped by a note
on the bottom space.
"Oh no!" exclaimed Tom
"I have a dilemma
we must go and see Luce
cause she is so clever."

Up the damp hill
they treaded and trudged
along the wet path
that had turned into sludge.

Arriving at the end
of Wildflower Lane
Luce welcomed them in,
"Come out of this rain."

Tom said, "Meet my friend,
Griffin the Gecko,
who just saved my life
with his small sticky toes.
He's lost his home,
could he stay with you?"
"Well I've got a spare place
on line number two."
So Griffin thanked Luce
for being so kind,
then found his new home
to relax and unwind.

"There's one other thing
I must ask of you."
I've found a note
that's left me confused."
D's on line 4,
C's on space 3,
A's on space 2,
then this NEW note you see.
It lives' on space one
and appears very low.
What letter could it be?
I just do not know."
"Not to worry." said Luce
"I have just the thing
to teach you the note
for the song you can't sing."

"Do you remember
Florence the Flea?
To learn the new note
well, SHE is the key."
Flo lives at the bottom
of the Treble Clef post

in space number one
she is the F note!"
"I've got it!" said Tom
"You've done it again"
now I will sing
For all of our friends."

Then Dylan zipped out,
Cadence grumped around
Aria danced a jig
Flo bounced to the sound
Tom serenaded
the sweetest of tunes
whilst all the bugs danced
the whole afternoon.

Tom thanked everyone
for saving the day
he bid them farewell
and set off on his way.
He strolled down the path
singing the tune,
all the way back
to Kent's Lagoon.

Ickle Ockle

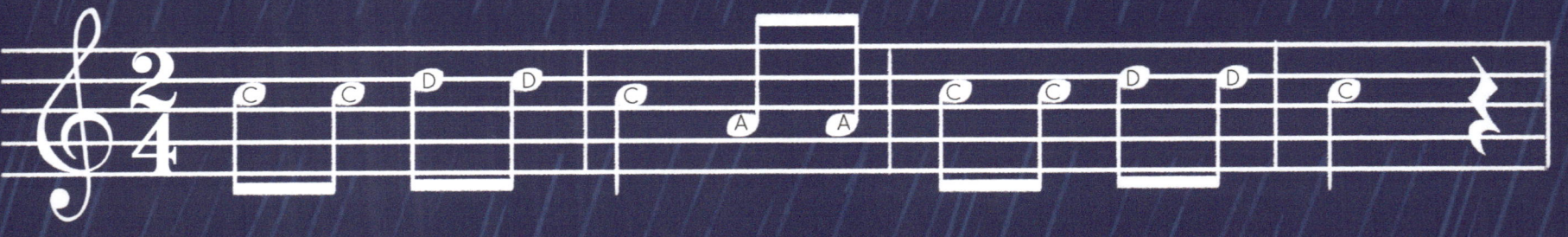

Ick-le Ock-le blue bo-tle, fish-es in the sea,

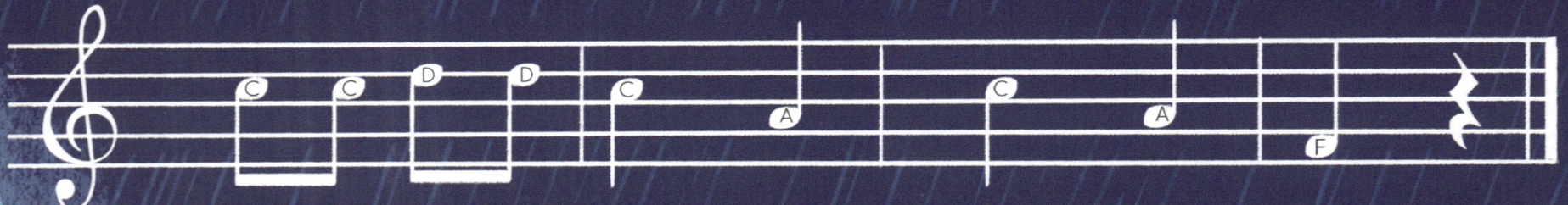

If you want a part - ner, please choose me.

ABOUT

*"Music evokes; music suggests; music implies, and music opens up the mind of
a child in an extraordinary way."*
Richard Gill.

Music education is unparalleled in its ability to foster patience and resilience while at the same time opening the mind to creativity and imagination. My hope in writing this series of books is that they would bridge the gap from solfège to reading letter names through the guise of storytelling.

To aid children's recollection of the story and support the learning outcomes, I have also included some free resources such as an mp3 of the song 'Ickle Ockle.' These resources can be found at www.jaischelbach.com.

It doesn't matter how you use this book or how old you are. If the story reaches into your heart and moves you, then this is the first step to understanding the power of a story and the heartbeat of music. May you always keep singing, learning, and growing so that the beauty of music continues to pass from one generation to the next!

JAI SCHELBACH

Jai grew up in the Scenic Rim area of South East Queensland and has many fond memories of living in Kalbar and Boonah. In 2005, he finished his Bachelor Music/Bachelor Education degree at UNSW. He currently lives on the Gold Coast and teaches music to students from Kindergarten through to Grade 5.

ANDRÉS GONZÁLEZ

Andrés was born on the east side of Colombia. After obtaining his Bachelor Degree in Graphic Design, he decided to specialize in telling stories through illustration. Today he lives in Amsterdam and enjoys creating storybooks for children.

www.ingramcontent.com/pod-product-compliance
Lightning Source LLC
Chambersburg PA
CBHW050854010526

44107CB00048BA/1606